J. W. and Me

The Small Town Texas Experience

Barbara V. Montgomery

HERITAGE BOOKS
2007

HERITAGE BOOKS
AN IMPRINT OF HERITAGE BOOKS, INC.

Books, CDs, and more—Worldwide

For our listing of thousands of titles see our website
at
www.HeritageBooks.com

Published 2007 by
HERITAGE BOOKS, INC.
Publishing Division
65 East Main Street
Westminster, Maryland 21157-5026

Copyright © 2007 Barbara Venton Montgomery

Other books by the author:
Lovinia's Child: A Depression Tale
Wonderful "Wicked" Women of the World
Women Short-Changed by History

All rights reserved. No part of this book may be reproduced or transmitted in any form or by any means, electronic or mechanical, including photocopying, recording or by any information storage and retrieval system without written permission from the author, except for the inclusion of brief quotations in a review.

International Standard Book Number: 978-0-7884-3759-5

For J. W Cullins, an honorable peace officer who taught me the difference between the law and justice.

And always, for Melody and Melinda.

Thank you to my adopted God children who have delighted my life when the twins went away; Meg, Dr. Ted Switzer, Wally, Bic, John and Jim.

* * *

For those persons who helped in the preparation of the book:
Hallie Garner
Bette Moscarello
Sam Buffington
Mary Hanrahan
Mary Ann Asberry
Carol Moton Hawkins
Inez Gipson
Thank you.

The names of living persons are withheld or changed to protect the guilty.

J. W. and Me: The Small Town Texas Experience

Explanation...

J. W. and Me: The Small Town Texas Experience

This reminiscence began as a light-hearted account of dispensing justice in a very small Texas town in the early 70's. Everyone knew their neighbors, the Saturday night drunk, the wife-beater, the pilferer, the runaway, the adulterer and all the other not-too-honest and honest citizens residing in any small town. The town remained that way for a brief period even after the lake was born out of the east branch of the Trinity River.

What was it like before this climactic occurrence? In researching background material, there was a darker picture that emerged. It was "the lynching." This could have been the history of other towns across the South, building up to the year of 1919; the year of the most lynchings in the United States. The smallest county in the state of Texas, Rockwall, did not escape.

The problem for the researcher was that no one wanted to talk about "the lynching" that took place in Rockwall in 1909. The old courthouse had burned; Rockwall had withdrawn from Kaufman County and no one in the twenty first century would discuss this terrible crime. But it happened, and the memory had not gone away, because phone calls were abruptly ended and old friends shied away from commenting. But "the lynching" is part of the history of race relations in Rockwall county which has been ignored.

As a former officer of the court, who learned from J. W. Cullins the difference between the law and justice, the lynching in Rockwall was like a boil that needed to be lanced. What had happened in 1909? Did anyone try to prevent this horror? Did people see themselves in that mirror of events?

With the help of articles from the archives of *The Dallas Morning News* and grown-up children and grandchildren who had listened to the fractured accounts of the events, "the lynching" had to be included in the book. It became the first chapter along with other occurrences that are Rockwall County's heritage, and background material for the book about dispensing justice in Rockwall.

The Statue of Justice is shown with a blindfold covering her eyes. Who put it there? Was it done in the past, similar to the draping of her breasts by an "offended Attorney General?" The scales she holds appear to be balanced. Does this mean she has no opinion and hopes that someone else will bear witness to the truth?

J. W. and Me: The Small Town Texas Experience

J. W. Cullins, Chief of Police, Heath, Texas. He lived by his motto: "Do the right thing." *Courtesy of John Cullins.*

PART I

"To the living, one owes consideration;
To the dead, only the truth."

Voltaire
(Lettres Sur Oedipe)

J. W. and Me: The Small Town Texas Experience

Everything changed in our small county when the lake filled up. It happened quickly in 1970. It rained, it poured and water ran off the hills into the east fork of the Trinity River to form Lake Ray Hubbard. There had never been so much rain, and people around the lake considered acquiring boats to float off of their property as the rain continued. Earth movers, cars, trees disappeared into the quickly rising water. And still it rained. Flying above the lake today, you can still see the yellow Caterpillar tractors left behind as homes for fish.

No one was blamed for the equipment loss; nor do most people recall the man for whom the lake was named. Who was he? What did he do? When the governments, state or federal, decided that a lake was good for "progress" and politicians, there was a lake. As they say in Washington, D.C., an honest politician is one who has been bought and stays bought. So his loyalty deserves his name on a park, street, freeway, airport, lake, etc.

Still, even with the population and the "progress," some residents of the county missed "the good old days" before the lake, when the river bottom was home to wolves, foxes, mink (yes, mink) skunks, coyotes, raccoon, deer, wild turkey and an old black bear. There were remains of Indian weirs covered by the water, but no Indians.

Some folks say that prehistoric man, or an ancient tribe, built the meandering rock wall for which the county and city were named. However, geologists, who arrive from time to time to study the wall, say this is nonsense. It is a natural formation. Archaeologists have pointed out that no artifacts have been found to indicate that prehistoric man was ever involved with the rock wall, despite one small stone serpent's head found by Dr. Glenn many years ago. This has not prevented some Dallas "businessmen" from bringing people out to see the famous rock wall. A small box lunch and a blanket to cover the fire ant mounds were included in the price of the excursion.

In very ancient times, the Rockwall area had been part of a large inland lake left behind by glacial melt. Prehistoric monsters of one kind or another lived here. Residents have found vertebrae washed up along the lakeshore and verified by anthropologists as proof of their existence.

Maybe the monsters ate the Indians who supposedly built the rock wall.

* * *

J. W. and Me: The Small Town Texas Experience

In the years after the Civil War, farmers and ranchers needed workers in the cotton fields. Where to find them? The Settlement. Where I-30 meets Ridge Road and 740, or Ridge Road, there was a thriving community with a church, homes, a cemetery and black citizens who picked and farmed cotton. All of the land for a mile in all four directions was owned by black families. Some of this land is still owned by these families; some has been taken by eminent domain or sold to developers for roads to be built to the chain stores and restaurants along I-30 and Ridge Road. Gradually the town of Rockwall pushed south. As this happened, racial tensions were apparent.

A day of planting in early Rockwall. *Courtesy of Rockwall Historical Foundation.*

Before the lynching in 1909, the county had problems. The archives *of The Dallas Morning News* show a record of raids on "colored" homes, mob violence and the "whitecaps."

Where the "whitecaps" got this name is not

revealed—maybe they wore white caps as opposed to the white sheets of the Klan. They dynamited homes of black citizens, forcing the families to run for their lives.

The headlines from *The Dallas Morning News* indicate the mayor of Rockwall was so concerned that he called a mass meeting on August 24, 1898 to denounce the "whitecaps." The meeting collected $250.00 for the "apprehension and conviction of the guilty parties."

On the streets and in the stores of Rockwall, there was "great indignation" and a demand for quick riddance of these unknown characters. There is no evidence that the money was ever awarded, although it was hoped that "Rockwall must retain her character hitherto known for morality and the obedience to law."

Before the tragic events of March 1909 there was a "debate of the race problem" in Waco in January 1906 at Baylor University. W.I. Lofland of Rockwall won first place. "Industrial education of the Negro" seems to have been the topic of the "interesting" discussions, according to *The Dallas Morning News*.

But the hate of the "whitecaps" and an underlying not-so-subtle prejudice of some citizens in Rockwall are evidenced by the events recorded by the paper on March 7, 1909. The violence was so overwhelming that no one in the 21st century with any knowledge or pictures of the event would talk about it.

The headlines in *The Dallas Morning News* were: "Mob Burns Man at Stake," "People Overrule Authorities at Rockwall and Prisoner is Killed." Charged with "attempted" (quotes mine) criminal assault upon a white woman, Anderson Ellis was dragged from the Rockwall jail at night by a gang of men who said "that any attempt to thwart the will of the crowd would meet with summary vengeance."

Courtesy of Rockwall Historical Foundation.

The word had gone out to insure that there would be a crowd in Rockwall the next day. The reporter estimated that approximately 1000 people from Dallas, Collin and Hunt counties arrived to witness the lynching.

"No rowdyism would be permitted," was the order of the mob.

Earlier, the preceding day, before these "rowdies" had located Ellis, Andrew Clark had refused their search of his house, so they killed his son.

When members of the mob found Ellis in jail, did they overpower the sheriff—or did he relinquish the keys and watch the lynching from a prominent spot on the second floor of a building overlooking the town square? Where the United States flag waves today in the heart of Rockwall was the place of the lynching.

It was there that Ellis was "secured to a large iron stake driven into the earth; cordwood was saturated with kerosene and piled about him." Before the torch was applied, he was questioned by the leader of the mob. He admitted the "attempted" attack to his accuser, but refused to make any further statements.

"The torch was then applied." He quickly burned. Did he scream as the flames seared his flesh? Did the thousand cheer as they watched a man burn to death?

The paper reported that "the crowd then dispersed," and the night's stillness was unbroken.

Old Courthouse of Rockwall County, Texas, built in 1892.
Courtesy of Rockwall Historical Foundation.

***

Forty years later, *The Dallas Morning News* reported that Dallas had become "a trading point for farmers in the area." However they needed workers "desperately" and were paying $2.00 for 100 pounds of picked cotton.

Rockwall County had changed little over the years. Ladies drove their carriages down dirt roads to the Trinity River bottoms to fish and picnic under the watchful eyes of their escorts. Some even lifted their skirts to go wading in the muddy waters. Well-to-do cotton farmers built three-story wooden houses with stained glass windows and the requisite storm cellar for emergencies, and their wives canned beans, corn, cucumbers and preserves.

For several decades there were a few disruptions in this bucolic atmosphere.

However, in 1959 in the Federal District Court, several peace officers pled guilty to violating the civil rights of a farm hand. They were accused of forcing him to work for them to pay off a $15 debt. This was a form of "debt peonage" that had been practiced in Texas for many years. If a black farmer owed a debt to his employer, his labor could be sold to another employer for the amount of the debt, plus interest. The black farmer would then work for his new employer until the original debt, plus interest, was paid. Or he might even be sold again to another employer to pay for the accumulated debt.

The sheriff was also accused of taking prisoners out of the jail during an election to vote for him. As an election judge, I was asked by several parents in 1976 why they couldn't take a ballot to the jail for their son. The sheriff had always permitted it. Was I sure this couldn't be done?

In 1958 came *Brown vs. the Topeka Board of Education* which ended segregation in the public school system. The decision prompted a whole new debate in Rockwall County, this time in Royse City, between a young Methodist minister and the principal of the high school.

The young minister was quoted in *The Dallas Morning News* as saying, "If anyone wants an example of unequal facilities, we have it here. During the 105-degree summer days, a barrel of ice water was furnished to the Negro pupils. A hundred and fifty of them shared four tin cups. There is no inside plumbing. Privies are located a few steps from the main building."

The high school principal in Royse City agreed that better facilities were needed, "but I'm strictly against mixing whites and blacks."

He said his students agreed with him. "Just like a dictatorship," he accused President Eisenhower for sending troops to Selma to integrate the university there.

Rockwall had done better. New buildings housing the Bourn Avenue School had been constructed. They are still used today by factories and shops. The school had a gym, track, and inside plumbing. In the Southside, students wanted to keep their school. However, during the summer, the board of education, prompted by the mayor, sold the entire facility to a private investor and there was no choice but to integrate.

When citizens of The Settlement in the late 1960's were informed that Lake Ray Hubbard would take most of their property, they began leaving their homes. Farmers dispersed; some went to Dallas, some to Southside in Rockwall, and others just left for other parts.

The Cedar Grove Church moved up on the hill overlooking I-30 and Horizon Road.[1]

The historic Glen Hill Cemetery became surrounded to the South by homes and to the East by development along Ridge Road. and The Settlement disappeared into Lake Ray Hubbard and almost from Rockwall history.[2]

Another opportunity for progress in Rockwall came in the 1970's when the state decided to relieve north/south traffic in Rockwall as Dallas spilled to the

---

[1] See Appendix I.

[2] See Appendix II.

east.

Why not run the six-lane by-pass in Rockwall through the Southside community and make the right-of-way commercial? The planning and zoning commission and the city council (all white) decided this was a great idea and perfect for "progress."

Before the final determination was made, the word spread throughout the town. A few of the descendants of those who decried the "whitecaps" and newer residents with friends in Southside organized. The entire community and their supporters engulfed the courtroom on a Thursday night in old city hall where the P&Z sat. Crying babies, small yapping dogs, young and old took every seat and leaned on the four walls. The effect of all those black faces was stunning. The decision to commercialize Southside reversed and the bi-pass went away to be fought over another day.

* * *

Driving across Lake Ray Hubbard today and seeing the marinas, parks and expensive homes, it is difficult to conceive of the racial problems, and also of the fight that had precipitated the coming of the lake. Although Rockwall County did multiply after the lake splashed its western shores, some citizens missed the cotton culture economy; some were afraid of losing their income and their prestige as landed gentry.

Certain families were ensconced and county offices were almost hereditary. Although political parties changed in the 1980's and the party of "self interest" (self described) took over, allegiances seldom changed.

The once small towns of Royse City, Fate and Heath grew apace with Rockwall. What had been one county now became a county of small growing towns whose citizens still referred to their residences as being in Rockwall.

J. W. and Me: The Small Town Texas Experience

PART II

"Here comes de judge;
Here comes de judge."
Amos and Andy

J. W. and Me: The Small Town Texas Experience

When I moved to Heath, in Rockwall County in 1969, there was one housing development of Candlelight Park and four houses in Cove Ridge which were south of I-30. There were still raccoons, deer, fox, one grey wolf and plenty of skunks who had invaded my house when it stood empty. The skunks were quite friendly. They would "put forth" only when the doorbell rang or when they heard a strange voice at the door, which was often. They liked the attic, and they would face me down if I climbed the stairs to see what they were doing. Clothes smelled of skunk. When I went out, friends would whisper in my ear, trying not to get too close, "Skunk."

The eight skunks had to go. Along the foundation I put out a mixture of eggs and milk hoping to coax them out of the house. Four exterminators tried, they departed but the skunks remained. Finally, the fifth and last exterminator brought his brother with him on their way to go night fishing. They never made it. The brother got so sick of the smell that he just lay out on the grass by the driveway and became violently sick.

His only printable comment was, "That's the biggest damn skunk I ever saw."

I hated to kill granddaddy skunk, but he and I couldn't live in the same house. The atmosphere and my wardrobe improved considerably when he left. I could apply for a teaching job without apologizing for the scent I created.

* * *

Heath, at the southern end of Rockwall County, had a population of 75 in 1892. By the 1970's the sign at FM 1140 read population 1172. Heath had a general store and a small strip center where the city council met. In the old school, a block down the road, was a large room attached to the fire station for community events. It was a wonderfully typical small town.

When the town finally had a population of 1500, the Texas law stated that the city council must have a municipal judge. No longer could the mayor act in that capacity because of a possible conflict of interest. The job required citizenship, good moral character and the advanced age of 21.

At a city council meeting on a Thursday night, the mayor and one councilman were absent. This left a quorum of three to do the monthly business, one member being the first woman elected to the council in Heath. "How about it?" she asked me. "I have two votes, mine and a friend of yours. Let's surprise the mayor." I won the secret ballot for municipal judge 2 to 1. It certainly was a surprise to all, including me.

The court at that time was held in the city council room, part of the small commercial strip center. What was needed to run a court? I certainly didn't know. With the help of Aileen Terry, the city secretary, we bought a new docket book, the United States flag, a stand for the flag and a city seal because all discussions of the court had to be recorded and sealed.

The chief of police was J. W. Cullins. He had one deputy, one car and the help of his son, Doug Cullins, a constable for the county. J. W. was unsure about the judge he was inheriting with good reason.

I had been in court once in my life and that was a custody case when I was five years old. I wet my panties, cried, and was removed from the witness stand and had become a ward or the court, entering foster care. I had watched court cases on television and had read the history of municipal courts, beginning with the Bow Street Runners in London. Incidentally, this was a volunteer job, no money involved, so no one really wanted to be judge. When I left the court after nine years, there were 52 applicants for the job and a citation for being one of the best small courts in Texas, all because of J. W.

J. W. and Me: The Small Town Texas Experience

*　*　*

J. W. Cullins had experience in law enforcement. He had been a prison guard at Huntsville, but in 1940 he had returned home and bought a farm in Heath where he was born. He became the first chief of police of the town, but he always called himself a peace officer, and he didn't *police* as much as *keep the peace*. He taught me that common sense was more important than a law degree.

It wasn't until he was in the nursing home and legally blind that I learned he carried his beloved five-string banjo with him. He loved to play the banjo and guitar at pick-up sessions with Harley Dobe and Dale Watkins, fiddlers. They were joined by Hardy Mays, Mattie's husband, who could play anything. They would go around Rockwall county entertaining at dances and barbeques. That must have been why he knew everyone; parents, grandparents, children and dogs.

He found wayward children and brought them home. He admonished mayors who beat their wives. He drove drunken young men home and lectured them and their parents, saving those who would have been charged with a DWI or public intoxication. He did not police; he kept the peace. He saved me from being a bad judge. I later received a commendation from the

J. W. and Me: The Small Town Texas Experience

Municipal Courts Association because of his judgment and common sense. I was always asked at the meetings of the Municipal Courts' Association why there were only two appeals in nine years from the court.

"When J. W. Cullins brings them in, they are guilty, no doubt about it."

After my "election" as judge, J. W. called the next day to introduce himself and officially inform me as to the court dates and procedures. He was very formal. I called him Mr. Cullins and he called me Mrs. Montgomery. We spoke about our concerns, the court and many other things. After that conversation, he called me Miss Barbara but I always called him Mr. Cullins. He was the most honest man I have ever met. When a young deputy picked up J. W.'s granddaughter for speeding, he was disappointed with me because I gave her a driver's education course instead of a fine. As a first offender, I had to offer her this option. He wanted her to understand that the law was applicable to her, too.

If I made a decision that city officials didn't like, or their friends complained about traffic tickets, J. W. Cullins would say, "You did the right thing."

* * *

J. W. and Me: The Small Town Texas Experience

My first day was a memorable experience. In the one-room council chambers with one big table, the city was sponsoring a dog clinic with free shots for rabies and distemper. The dogs, howling and afraid, were at one end of the table and I was holding court at the other end. A young man from Dallas had a speeding ticket. To approach my end of the table, he had to go around dogs, big dogs, little dogs, medium sized dogs, pulling at their leashes and barking frantically at one another. I have never seen a person as terrified as my speeder. He trembled all over; his eyes rolled back in his head. I thought he would faint when he grabbed a chair and was violently ill all over the floor, causing the dogs to bark even louder. What to do? I had no idea I would be sharing the small room with dogs. I love dogs and had four at this time, but I learned that day that some people really fear them.

I dismissed my first case and had to call his friend to take him home. My court had *really* gone to the dogs.

My second case gave me a feeling that I was really the judge in this courtroom:

We had an old bridge over a stream that ran into the lake. It was too narrow to park on, but some people would sit in their cars on the bridge and fish from there in defiance of NO PARKING signs at either end of the bridge. Once a character from Terrell never heeded these warning signs and almost blocked the bridge with his car. Of course, J. W. got him and brought him into court. He took one look at the one-room, one table court and me in jeans and a T-shirt and said, "What kind of rinky-dinky court is this?"

Bad choice of words.

It was hot that day and we had no fan nor air conditioner. Since the city council met only once a week and at night, the councilmen had no need to spend money on a fan.

The irate citizen should have stopped commenting then, and his fine would have been $5.00, but he continued:

"Can't you people afford a fan, and why can't I park on that rinky-dinky bridge, anyway?"

He seemed to like those words. His fine went up to $15.00.

"You can't do that to me." I could, and I did. His fine was now $25.00.

"Who do you think you are?"

I replied, "I am the judge and your fine has doubled to $50.00. Keep talking." He did. When he stopped, I had fined him $75.00 and threatened him with contempt of court and three days in jail.

That did it, finally. As he stomped out, he held the door open and yelled to me, "It's still a rinky-dinky court."

We had his money, and J. W. smiled. After that, I wore my doctoral robe to court.

Another time we were lucky when it came to one stolen car. Billy Peoples, who sold used cars in the town of Rockwall, called to say that a customer had come in to buy a good used car.

"He left his junker here and took off heading south. I want my car returned. Pick that @#$%&* up!" J.W was on patrol and he caught the car thief going through Heath. He brought him in. Sure enough, he answered the description of the thief and J. W. took him to the Rockwall County jail. Billy Peoples got his car returned.

The jail in Rockwall left much to be desired. It was on the third floor at the top of the art-deco city hall. On the first floor was the police station; on the second floor was the county courtroom; third floor was the jail. But often during county court, you could hear the inmates yelling at one another and at the jailor. The windows were open except on very cold days, so the inmates would call out to people on the square, "Hey you, get me out of here."

"Bring me some booze," which a jailor got caught doing.

"Pretty thing, need a date?" and other very crude remarks.

The Rockwall County Courthouse/City Hall/County Jail. Note the windows at the top of the building where inmates would call down to pedestrians. *Courtesy of Mary Hanrahan.*

There are new jail facilities now, and political receptions are held at the old courthouse.

* * *

Guns are part of Texas culture. In the 70's, there were gun racks in every pickup along with old beer cans on the floor. J. W. knew there were dangerous men who would sometimes be brought into court.

"Miss Barbara, you need a gun, not a little peashooter, but a police special. We'll go to Town East and find you a 38."

At the gun shop J. W. gave me my choice of three guns. I must have picked the right one because he nodded his approval. So I acquired a gun to carry in my purse or in the glove compartment. I took it with me to court. J. W. taught me how to use that gun by setting up beer cans behind the old Heath cemetery and having me blast away until I could knock them off the fence post.

I pulled the gun out only once when I planned to shoot two stalkers who wanted to steal my car. I'm a bad shot. They ran for their lives. Good thing. I later sold it to a Rockwall deputy and earned a blue belt in Karate instead.

When I first met Mattie Mays, one of the first women justices-of-the-peace in East Texas, she hauled a big gun out of the huge purse she carried and announced, "Honey, I'm never without it. I'm called in the middle of the night to look at corpses, and having that big "ole" gun gives me comfort." When the first accused rapist appeared before me in court one night, I knew exactly what she meant.

Mattie also married people. I hoped I could do this because I was asked often enough, but city judges were not permitted, so I sent friends to Mattie and wrote out their vows in my fractured Spanish.

When I met Fairy Watson, Mattie's mother, at a senior lunch, she was a tiny, beautiful fairy dressed up in flowered dress, carrying little white gloves. She asked for a ride home in that big, red convertible. That began a wonderful friendship I cherish to this day.

Each Friday in the nursing home, we had picnics and ice cream socials, political discussions, philosophical arguments and I renewed my love for the grandparents I barely remembered from foster care. I could tell her anything and she listened with bright, understanding eyes. I don't know how old she was, but she was my dearest friend.

* * *

In one of the funniest hearings of the court, J. W. Cullins brought in a couple, very drunk, dancing in the road, singing ribald songs and enjoying themselves thoroughly. They joyfully admitted to being intoxicated. In their best interests they needed to go to jail and sleep it off. As J. W. was taking them out the door, the man happily asked for a favor. Could I put them in the same cell so they could continue to have a good time together? No, I explained, this was not possible. These were separate facilities for men and women.

"Oh well, ok, but one more favor judge. Please call my wife and tell her I'll be late coming home."

He forgot to give me her number.

After several years, J. W. hired a young man to replace him as chief of police, although he still worked every day. Ailene Terry was city secretary and also acted as court clerk. I did reports to the state and all of the paper work connected with the court. However, there were times when there was no one to act as bailiff and bring defendants into my room at the new city hall. Across the street from our facility lived my helper. After school, he would cross the road, eating cookies or a sandwich and escort people into court. Sometimes, there were men who had in the past committed serious crimes. One immigrant believed he was still fighting the Russians in his home in Hungary. As people waited in the new addition to the city hall, my assistant would call out their names and lead them into my office. Everyone was startled to see a 10 year-old with a badge over his heart, but I found him to be very dependable and helpful. I was sorry when he and his mother moved away. I think she may have been relieved.

Doug Cullins, J. W. 's son, and I often worked together on certain occasions. On July 4th we would ride together cautioning people who were lighting bottle rockets aimed at cedar shake roofs that caught fire easily. We confiscated enough fireworks that we had our own display on the weekend at J. W. 's little ranch house in the county. People would line up their cars along the road to see the show that was better than anything in Rockwall at that time.

One Fourth of July we were warned of a fight between two gangs coming out from Dallas to do battle by the lake. Terrell police said they would join us at the south end of the lake. This could be a dangerous situation. Doug was driving in place of J. W. that night when we got the call. I was told to carry my gun. I had left the gun at home because I was going to a party later. Dressed up in white slacks and purple silk blouse with dangling rhinestone earrings, I set out with Doug to stop a gang fight.

There were neither homes nor lights then at the southern end of the lake. It was pitch black. We didn't even see the cars by the side of the road until we were next to the first one. Several gang members were standing there swinging chains which caught the moonlight. The gangs were dressed in black. Doug left the headlights of the patrol car on and the shadows moved to the side of the dirt road. He got out his gun, and I got out of the car in my party clothes.

What does one say, outlined in the headlights of the police car, to gang members you cannot see?

"Hello, there."

No one moved. I announced to the shadows that I was the judge and late for my party. What was the problem? I don't know what would have happened if we hadn't seen the flashing lights of four patrol cars from Terrell coming around the lake toward our car.

The shadows moved at once into their cars. Without headlights, the gang cars moved quickly down the dirt road, turning left in the direction of I-30 which led into Dallas. When the Terrell police cars arrived, Doug and I were waiting for them.

"Where's the rumble," the sheriff in the first car asked Doug. He hadn't seen the nine cars without headlights leave the lake.

We just told them that they were too late for the action, and I was too late for the party. I always got scared after the fact.

When I was on a Fulbright to Israel, our limo was

hijacked by a Jordanian who wanted to go home. Two of us were taken on the road to Bethlehem as the Jordanian prepared to run the Allenby Bridge. Three jeep-like vehicles driven by armed Israelis pulled our limo off the road. I had been too busy at the time considering my escape options to worry about what might happen. It wasn't until I was returned to the guest kibbutz that I had the time to be scared. My roommate, Birdie, led me to our room when I realized there was a problem walking because my knees were shaking. That's really why I never went to the party. My knees were shaking.

J. W. and I had our share of inebriates, but only one gentleman who enjoyed his visits to court. He would present me with flowers that he had picked from those Ailene had planted beside the city hall. Waiting his turn for a hearing, he would play the old piano in the community room to great applause. He tipped the 10-year-old bailiff and greeted me happily. The suitcase he carried contained no papers, but a brand of every booze on the market.

"Would J. W. like a drink?"

"Would the judge like a cocktail?"

Since he was in no condition to drive, J. W. would see that his car made it home, and he got to jail.

We saw him regularly for a year. I hope he made it to rehab.

* * *

Acting as a magistrate, I could do all kinds of things like taking away a driver's license or committing people to the mental institution in Terrell. I never used this power. I could also jail someone for contempt of court which I threatened to do on occasion. This included several city council members. My tenure of office was not without a little controversy.

Neither J. W. Cullins nor I "fixed" tickets. We were not intimidated by the city fathers, some of whom expected us to uphold their interests. At one council meeting they debated my appointment, especially when a very wealthy man with an unreliable reputation thought I had too much power and wanted one of his cronies to take over.

A real problem began when Mr. Smith (not his real name) bought some property in the city. It had a large water tank on it built during the depression. No one knew how deep it was or if it held any secrets. Since Mr. Smith had small children, he considered the tank a danger to them. Other people had hoped to buy the property, but he outbid them. What a ruckus over that tank! It was like a sacred well. No one wanted it drained except the owner. Where would the water that was drained from it flow, onto other property? Wasn't it contaminated? Or was it that someone didn't want this man to be on that property?

I called the state health department and had the water tested. The city engineer checked the lay of the land to be certain the water would flow into the drainage ditch along highway 205. I called the state to see if there was any objection to this. But the only objection came from a few landowners and city officials. I received several unpleasant phone calls which could be defined as harassment. The Klan threatened to become involved. Critical letters to the editor appeared in the local paper to which, ethically, I could not respond. It was time to call in the Municipal Courts Association, headed at that time by Gary Bledsoe, a civil right lawyer.

He drove from Austin to Heath to lecture the city council on what could happen to them for pressuring/harassing a judge. He explained that unless they could prove I had committed moral turpitude, I was entitled to a public hearing and could put all of them in jail for three days for contempt of court.

It was tempting, but I declined. Instead I backed

Mr. Smith and told him he could drain the damned pond.

On that fateful Saturday morning, the entire town appeared to see the draining of the pond. What lay at the bottom of the murky waters? Treasure? Drugs? Forbidden cans of DDT? A stolen car or a skeleton?

Here was a mystery. The water slowly drained out of the tank for several hours. People ate their picnic lunches and watched. J. W. and I sat in his patrol car and drank coffee.

At last the water receded and all we could see at the bottom of the drained pond were several water-soaked boxes of old clothes.

Not a body; no treasure, just old, wet clothes. Disappointed, people drove their cars home and complained what a waste of time the whole morning had been.

I was grateful to Mr. Bledsoe and called him for advice several times. He always told me I was the autocrat of my court and, like J. W. , he would say, "Do the right thing."

I felt better about the Municipal Court Association after that. Attendance at their meetings for city judges was mandatory. Initially, the meetings of judges in Huntsville produced drunken oratory and misspelled fact sheets. Later, it became a learning experience with a state Supreme Court judge in attendance to explain the latest decisions of the court and how they affected local entities. After a three-day session, I would return to Heath, call in the part-time officers and inform them of what I had learned, reminding them to "show cause" when they came to court. The city paid my way because I received no salary for three years. Before I left the court, I was paid $300 a month.

When I went to Israel on my first Fulbright, I wrote my research paper comparing Israeli municipal courts to the Texas courts. In Texas you do not have to be a lawyer, but you must to go to judge school. Even the Constitution of the United States says nothing about being a lawyer as a requirement for sitting on the Supreme Court. Lawyers were mistrusted even in the eighteenth century. The members of the Knesset liked the paper and decided their judges could use more education after their life-time appointments, and they needed to be able to confer with one another from time to time.

Back in Texas, the lawyers who sat as judges always wanted to have separate sessions from their poor, non-lawyer, illiterate counterparts. Thirty years later, perhaps they have been successful in dividing the sheep from the goats. As J. W. said "its common sense not a law degree that counts."

J. W. and Me: The Small Town Texas Experience

PART III

"My object all sublime, I may achieve in time,
To let the punishment fit the crime,
 the punishment fit the crime."
The Mikado

J. W. and Me: The Small Town Texas Experience

There was no juvenile court in Rockwall County. By default, I was it. Most of the cases involved teenage drinking in the 70's—alcohol being the drug of choice. If parents and teachers were honest, it still is, along with meth.

Parents are required to be with their children when their cases are heard in court. It would have been easy to fine the kids for their misdemeanors, the parents would probably pay and that would be that. I chose the work route: wash the police cars, weed and plant flowers around city hall, clean the small park by the beach or go to Alcoholics Anonymous *with* a parent. This last requirement caused me problems with the city council when the co-captain of the football team and his father did not come to court. When they did not show up on their court date, J. W. said, "I'll go get them, they are at the high school football field."

And he did, interrupting football practice, absolutely unheard of in Texas.

The father was especially indignant. How could I stop football practice? Didn't I know the team was preparing for a big game? And his son hadn't been *that* drunk. And he certainly was not disturbing the peace.

He paid a fine for disorderly conduct and both father and son were ordered to a month of AA meetings. There were at least four meetings in that period. Out of city hall went papa and on the phone to council members, "Get rid of that judge."

Three months later I received a letter from the father. He apologized for his actions. He realized that *his* drinking was out of control, and he would be continuing to go to AA meetings. He thanked me, and said he had sent a copy of the letter to the city council.

The council members never acknowledged the letter. They were still upset over the harassment case and the draining of the tank, when they could have been confined in the Rockwall County jail for three days for contempt of court.

* * *

On another occasion a fifteen-year-old girl was drunk and couldn't run as fast as the other students when a high school party was raided. J. W. told me her single mother was more terrified than her daughter about what would happen in court. She had no extra money to pay a fine, and she was afraid of losing custody of her daughter.

J. W. always found out about things like that.

The daughter still looked drunk and was shaking

when she came to court. I delivered one of my few lectures on drinking. No, I mean I really stood up and yelled.

"If you are ever brought into this court again, I will see that you go to jail."

Eighteen years later, I was campaigning door-to-door. (I have run for everything except President of the United States and always lost.) The lady of the house opened the door, looked at me, smiled and said, "Bless you."

What a greeting for a would-be politician.

"You don't remember me." (I didn't)

"In twenty minutes you straightened out my daughter with a lecture that she has never forgotten. She is married now, with two children and is very happy. What are you running for? You have my vote."

How about that! Of course I lost the election, but the campaign was great.

* * *

I not only threatened to do things that a municipal judge can't do, but I did them. "Let the punishment fit the crime." Today, the State Commission on Judicial Conduct doesn't approve of "creative sentencing."

The *Rockwall County Herald Banner* ran a column

by John Browning who wrote about this oversight commission in Austin. It had publicly admonished a judge in Harris County for sentencing a woman to 30 days in jail on a restricted diet of bread and water for the first three days because she neglected two horses. This violated "Texas standards."

The district Judge in Rockwall told me that I couldn't do the things that I had done. Isn't that *ex post facto* or something? My guide in these matters was always J. W. and Isidore of Seville.

There are former Rockwall authorities who sometimes are reluctant to speak to me today. If their offspring parked next to the city hall and proceeded to celebrate graduation with a case of beer, they were caught by the ever-watchful J. W. The fine was based on the number of beer cans tossed out the window. Honor students should not litter the city hall parking lot.

In the past I have kept good company: marching with Martin Luther King in Los Angeles and Caesar Chavez in south Texas. I even ran for that sometimes confused outfit, the House of Representatives. I forced my opposition to return to Washington on Christmas to rewrite the GI Bill for Vietnam Veterans, giving them the educational benefits they deserved. A recognition of the women who flew planes for the army in World War II had been bottled up in committee for fourteen years. Out it came from the House Committee on Veterans Affairs, through both houses and signed by President Jimmy Carter. In the campaign, the old railroad line from Tyler through Greenville and Rockwall was discussed. It's still there and could be tied into DART for commuters from East Texas going in to Dallas

I lost the election, but I believed that I had won in many ways. As I traveled East Texas in a burned-out old "caddy," I ate well and made many friends.

* * *

J. W. 's kindness extended to many people in the county, especially Marina Oswald, the wife of the man accused of killing J.F.K. J. W. kept the wolves at bay. Newspaper and TV reporters would follow her when she gave an interview. J. W. would drive her to the TV station. He encouraged people to help her find work. I always wondered what kind of prison guard he had been.

Vandals are seldom caught in the act, but J. W. did it. He discovered three young men who had broken the NO TRESSPASSING signs on the property of J.E.R.

Chilton, III. What was I going to do about it? They and their fathers came to court. I ordered them to bring material for new signs, make them and put them up at the original site. Everyone was agreeable to this. Perhaps for the first time, the three men had an opportunity to work with their sons; all six became good friends and Mr. Chilton was satisfied.

This policy of replacement worked again when vandals were caught smashing post boxes along the rural routes. J. W. got 'em. Most of the boxes were in front of homes belonging to elderly women and widows, who didn't have the money to replace them. But the young men and their fathers did. They were so carried away with the jobs that they raked yards, cleaned up trash and cleared out garages for several months for the women. Everyone felt good about it.

Of course there were juvenile delinquents and adults who *acted* like juvenile delinquents. It was usually more difficult dealing with the adults with bad attitudes—although several young people couldn't understand why I was picking on them—like the eleven-year old marijuana grower. He brought three big pots home and presented them to his mother for Easter. She proudly placed them in the front casement window to catch the sun, not knowing that the pots did not contain Easter lilies. The police driving by spotted the marijuana but could not touch them without a search warrant. Then, I discovered the intricacies of writing a search warrant: on what street was the house; what color was it; the number of the house; where in the house was the drug; how was it placed; and on and on. I love the Constitution of the United States, and I am grateful for its safeguards. Too bad, government officials haven't read it, but then many of them can't read, or else they find lawyers trying to circumvent it.

The mother of the young drug dealer was appalled when the police served her with the search warrant, and confiscated the marijuana. How could I charge her? Harboring a criminal? Growing a controlled substance? After her son told us where he got the plants, she took him home and we did not see mother or son in court again.

Another time, a fourteen-year old was not so fortunate. He lied to me and he lied about a couple who tried to help him, and I caught him in the lie. I sent him to a special school set up for juveniles in Terrell where they lived and went to school until they could be returned to society. A few took advantage of the program; many of them ended in the criminal justice system.

J. W. and Me: The Small Town Texas Experience

The lake was a particularly tempting place to drink and do drugs. Sometimes people actually fished there. Law enforcement patrolled it, but at night, small planes with pontoons would land and offload drugs. At the downtown college, I taught one of those who was caught. He had the choice of sitting in a jail cell all day, or going to school part-time. He was almost thirty and really had a sick child. He had no health care and not enough money from a legitimate job to cover expenses. And he could fly. After two semesters of A's, I didn't hear from him again—I hope he was released from jail and that his life changed for the better.

I should mention that I taught full-time, had court on Friday nights and Saturdays and worked the swing shift at the aluminum plant in the furnace room five days a week. I loved the heat that the furnaces gave out in winter and I like to see the big ingots, a pearly pink, pulled from the molds. It was a dirty job, but when work ended at 11 p.m. I drove home, showered, washed my hair and laid out my clothes for school. The furnace room paid for my trips to Paris with a group of chefs from Dallas. We ate our way across France. It was a "larky" experience.

I got fired after the foreman of the furnace room went speeding through Heath on his way home. He arrived in court on Friday night and there I was presiding, not in my hard hat, steel-toed boots and jeans, but in my black doctoral gown with its blue velvet stripes on the sleeve. He did a double-take. I fined him the maximum amount knowing he would fire me the next day. Good thing that I had made enough money for Paris in the spring. The employment office called me in before work the next day. The clerk said I had lied on the application form. Not true. The company wanted to know about my education. Did I have high school? Yes. Did I have any college? Yes. That was it. No one asked me about degrees, so I didn't write them on the form. I did receive a turkey and a ham when I left the aluminum plant, but no severance pay.

* * *

A group of middle-school boys went to the beach with some high school freshmen to "horse around" and drink beer. When they got thirsty, they asked an older couple who was always fishing there for water and more beer. They were given water, but no beer and were warned about being under-age. The boys were told J. W. patrolled the beach and that they would probably get caught. When the youngest one, about

13, got home his mother smelled beer. She asked him where he got it and he accused the older couple of supplying him and his friends. Of course the husband and wife were picked up next day fishing at the lake. Everyone concerned had to appear in court. Since we seldom had a town attorney available and no one brought a lawyer, I did the questioning.

Mrs. "Fisher" cried and said they had befriended the boy when his parents weren't home. How could he lie about them? I asked him who and where his drinking buddies were. They were older and it was obvious that he was afraid they would "get" him. His mother, at first, castigated the Fishers then turned her anger on him. He was more afraid of his mother than his buddies, and finally told the truth, begging his parents not to beat him. This was one case where I ordered a large fine and an apology for the Fishers. The boy and his parents left court not looking at anyone.

J. W. said, "You did the right thing."

J. W. and I couldn't avoid problems with city officials although we tried. One mayor thought he could build a fence around his property that included the "take-line" in the lake. I don't know what he did for a living, but he usually spent his time preaching for us sinners to repent.

J. W. and Me: The Small Town Texas Experience

The city of Dallas sent him a notice that he could not build his fence into the lake. J. W. and I were asked to accompany Dallas officials sent to tear down his fence. When he came from his house and saw the bulldozer, J. W. and me, his language did not become a man of God. He said that he would sue the city of Dallas and everyone on his property, including J. W. and me. He did too, and the judge threw his case out of court in the autumn. For a while we were concerned and the council was upset, because the mayor's wife brought no more cookies to the council meetings. At the break in business there had always been cookies or cake and coffee. No more.

Many county and city officials today are lawyers. It isn't that I don't like lawyers, but many of them are arrogant and believe they know everything. That reminds me of my first trial where two lawyers squared off and it was my turn to keep the peace.

The case involved a young man who missed the curve as he came down FM 740 nearing the heart of Heath. It was the oldest section of town and the houses were small frame buildings, usually constructed by the older owners who lived there. When he landed on someone's front lawn and hit their front tree, he began a tirade of four letter words at the top of his

J. W. and Me: The Small Town Texas Experience

lungs at twelve o'clock at night, waking up senior citizens who had not heard such language since they were kids. They called the police. When J. W. and his deputy arrived, this young man was still calling everyone and everything about him very bad names and he was drunk too. J. W. took him home, discussed his language with his father and told him to get a lawyer. He was going to be charged with public intoxication, disorderly conduct, resisting arrest and using obscene language in public. There were plenty of witnesses. If found guilty on all charges, the fine would be close to $250.00

If you're innocent, get a lawyer. The guilty always do.

In a town of 1500, where do you get a jury? The tax rolls didn't help—those were working folk, paying taxes, listed there. Of course, J. W. knew where to find jurors. I needed at least nine for trial, although only six would serve on the jury. The domino shack behind Brady's store where men gathered every day to play 21 or 36, or something like that, was the place to find a jury. To my surprise, half the town showed up, all wanting to be jurors. After the lawyers selected six reasonably sane men and women and several alternates, we began. What evidence would come in or go out? Common sense. I had been advised that I ruled the courtroom. I had to tell the lawyers to sit down and shut up when they interrupted each other. They did, to my surprise. Witnesses were called to testify, cross examinations were courtly and the trial proceeded. One witness hesitated about what he had heard because he felt it couldn't be repeated in mixed company. I told him to whisper it to the jury and me. His lawyer did not complain, but I blushed.

There was no room for the jury to contemplate a decision in the small courtroom so they carried their chairs outside to the parking lot. They sat in a circle and spectators had to be at least fifteen feet away from them. No eavesdropping. Brady's brought coffee and donuts for them. This simple case should have taken little time to resolve, but the jurors, being the center of attention, had such a good time eating and probably drinking that the afternoon passed quickly. Five hours later, the jury brought in their chairs and returned the verdict of guilty on all counts. When could they be jurors again? Not soon, I promised myself.

Defendants always had the option of either having the judge decide the case or taking it to a jury. Having seen the jurors in action, most defendants in the future wanted the judge to hear their case. Two hundred and fifty dollars was the fine. Part of that could be paid with jail time. It was so ordered.

J. W. and Me: The Small Town Texas Experience

Part IV

"He who would bring home the wealth of the Indies must carry the wealth of the Indies with him."

Andalusian saying.

When my salary went from nothing to $200, then to $300, I began traveling several weeks a year. At Christmas, I would return to Mexico. In the quiet summer weeks, I went to Italy; England; Scotland; Ireland; the British West Indies; Montserrat before the volcanic eruption; Greece to see Agamemnon's throne room; the former Yugoslavia, escaping just before the Serbs bombed Dubrovnik.

I had been excavating a 13th century church there with the nuns. They got me out of Dubrovnik before the ancient harbor walls were destroyed. While in Bosnia, I went to Medjigorie where children climbing the rocks to retrieve their sheep, saw a vision of the Virgin. She came to them pleading for peace. As Yugoslavia later descended into civil war and genocide as practiced by the Serbs, I wondered what she would think of the situation. In the ten days I spent in Yugoslavia, I never heard the laughter of children. Did they have a premonition of the slaughter that was to come?

I traveled to Egypt to see Hatshepsut's temple so I could write about her. Until then I had seen Deir el Bahri only in pictures that seemed haunting and mysterious. Who was the woman who had inspired a temple of such beauty of design? Several statues of

J. W. and Me: The Small Town Texas Experience

Hatshepsut are in the British Museum, but it is not easy to discern from them how this delicate woman, who became a pharaoh, could put on the crown of upper and lower Egypt and rule for twenty years, only to disappear into history. Her mummy has never been found.

I went Belgium to the finishing school for diplomats of the European Community; Spain, and the haunting Alhambra where Washington Irving wrote his tales and the spirit of El Cid lurks; Switzerland; Hong Kong before the British departed; and Singapore, the cleanest country in the world; Brazil with its black jaguars and anacondas.

I was served tea and cucumber sandwiches at the Grisham Hotel in Dublin when the riders came in for their sherry after a fox hunt. I've always felt sorry for the fox—too uneven a match. Passing through London many times, I went to all of the historic places about which I had taught students—the Tower where Ann Boleyn lost her head, Johnson's ancient pub, Parliament, and the British Museum.

Every Central American ruin that had been excavated—Copán, Tikal, Chichen-Itzá, Palenque and especially Monte Alban and Tula— was explored.

Something exciting always happened when I

traveled to Central America.

In Costa Rico, the whole country was shaking when Dr. Ted and I exited the plane. Later, the volcano erupted and we watched from a distance the hot, molten lava crawl down the volcano. At night, the atmosphere was a deep red as the yellow and orange magma moved toward the village at the foot of the volcano. Costa Rica is one country where you can drink the water from the taps everywhere.

In Guatemala, where we had gone to see the Mayan city of Tikal, we were unaware of the military takeover at the time. As we strolled down the empty street looking for an open restaurant, along came a big army tank with a revolving gun turret. Everything was closed except the hotel and its facilities. People crowded into the lobby looking for protection. Then we knew there was a military coup.

Not to be discouraged by this, we went on to Antigua by renting a small bus. The driver carried a machine gun, a hand gun and a machete. He told us that he would run all roadblocks and to keep our heads down when he ordered us to. We were not stopped on our way to Antigua, but later, after renting a car, we took the bus driver's advice, running two roadblocks and never looking back. No one came after us.

We flew into the airport in Tikal. There is no more magnificent ruin than Tikal. One section has been preserved just as the archeologists found it. Walking through that area is like swimming at the bottom of a lush, green ocean with the water surrounding you and waving seaweed blocking your way. The atmosphere is heavy and moist, making breathing difficult. Vine-covered ruins emerge in the half-dusk, mysterious and commanding. It is a wondrous place.

Palenque, in Mexico, is a small jewel of a ruin. Monte Albon is a place of space and quiet. Chichen-Itzá is almost a clash between Toltec and Mayan, but Tikal is a city, powerful and awesome.

On a trip to Honduras, we went to see Copán, a southern Mayan ruin outside of San Pedro Sula. Fifteen years later I had a teacher exchange to the college in San Pedro Sula, and the city and the ruin had changed dramatically. This time paid guides cornered tourists; before three small children were eager to show us their ruin.

Copán had expanded as the excavations uncovered homes of nobles and priests who buried their own under the foundations of the buildings—an unhealthy thing to do in times of sickness.

But it was the Honduran city of the Pedro Sula that

had changed so much. Armed guards were everywhere, even at the ice cream shop, at the restaurants and at the stores.

Fourteen armed guards covered everything at the bank. No credit cards were accepted. Travelers checks took four hours to cash, because they had to be cleared in Tegulcigapa. There were long lines at the bank and chairs to one side for those fortunate to have travelers checks.

Shopping for groceries in the morning required two armed guards. No woman was seen on the street without a male escort. One afternoon, as I was coming from the college, there was a shoot-out on the main street. We hunkered down in the van and prayed a stray shot wouldn't hit the gas tank. Not until I returned home did I find the state department report warning that Honduras was one of the three most dangerous places for U.S. citizens to visit.

Since teachers in public schools were on strike, we were taken to the Catholic University in San Pedro at 7:00 a.m. where two of us taught English to the staff. This was on their own time. Fourteen of them consistently showed up every morning. We awarded stars for attendance and performance. The fourteen vied to see who could get the most stars on their cards. They made the exchange worthwhile in spite of the danger.

* * *

Everywhere I traveled in the world was exciting and wonderful except Korea. My three favorite countries were New Zealand, Scotland and Morocco. Mexico is like a second home so it isn't included in the three.

I went to Morocco to see the Casablanca of Bogart and Bergman. What I found was the desert. The Sahara is an eternal sea in which it would be easy to lose oneself. It is timeless. It was like seeing the Grand Canyon for the first time. I joined a small group that was camping in the Sahara for five days. In the morning I would find a basin of warm water beside the tent flap and a small cup of green tea. Breakfast was cooked outside on a small stove. Then we walked to an oasis where the Tuareg, (blue men of the desert) would come to the well to water their camels. Each tribe had its own colored rope for the containers bringing up the water.

As we drove across the desert, our Land Rover broke down. Instead of waiting for the other vans to come, I rode a camel to the next campsite. This nasty, smelly animal hated me on sight and tried to bite me.

J. W. and Me: The Small Town Texas Experience

But I got on board. When we went up a dune, I hung on to her neck. When going down the dune, I grasped her tail and leaned back so I wouldn't fall head first going down. Lordy! What an experience! I hated her as much as she hated me. Before we returned to civilization, the drivers dressed me like a Tuareg woman. I could have joined a caravan and no one could have known the difference.

One late night a large caravan, coming over a ridge of dunes, was outlined by the full moon. I seriously considered following it and the comet, Hal Bop, streaking across the African sky.

* * *

On my first trip across the Atlantic, I met my best friend, Viva. We ate strawberries and ice cream across Spain and never stopped talking. People assumed we had known each other forever. She has been gone for a decade, but like Melody and Melinda, I miss her every day.

Next, I flew to Italy to join Loyola alumni on the top of Monte Mario, one of Rome's seven hills. A Dominican nun cleaned my room, and a Franciscan took me to Gandolfo where, in the Pope's courtyard, little Andalusian princesses danced for him. He blessed us all and floated back into his summer residency.

Of course, I tossed coins in the Trevi fountain. I stood in the ancient forum where Brutus began, or finished, the killing of Caesar. I marveled at the gold room of Etruscans, such jewelry design and beauty in gold. It had to have been copied from Sumer. Special permission from the mayor of Rome was required to enter the vault, but a kind doctor from Dallas and his wife declared I was his sister, and along with the necessary bribes, we all were admitted.

I hiked the Great Wall of China and explored the Forbidden City. The last dowager empress of China, at some point, parted with a red dragon robe which is now mine.

On an exchange with the Maoris, I slept on mats, nose to nose with strangers. I traveled with them by bus to the river of the green stones, went whale watching in the Northern Antarctic, and learned to smother everything, including green beans, with whipped cream. I dined with the Maori queen at her invitation. Her guests are required to sing for their supper. I rendered the *Eyes of Texas Are Upon You*—it was awful, but she laughed. The French Consul refused to sing. I offered to help, but he had just heard me sing and refused my help. However, I was taken to the

Queen's treasure room filled with decorated green stones and gifts from other monarchs and governments, while he had to sit outside. When I had an asthma attack, she sent me to her doctor for herbs and massage.

I loved these gracious, hospitable people who, at one time, ate their captives. They understood my Shawnee heritage so I was considered "a person of the earth." Their aristocracy tattooed, so they appreciated my tattooed butterflies.

Israel, before the Intifada, seemed to be a safe place. I visited all of the municipal courts, walked the wall that circles all of Suleman's Jerusalem, climbed Masada and stood on the ruins of Megedo, looking down on the valley of Armageddon where the world will end. Several battles have been fought there, from ancient times to World War I. At dusk, when the wind picks up the dust, in its whirls one can envision soldiers and chariots clashing in the coming darkness. But in Qumran there is peace and quiet.

Leaving the kibbutz with a small group for a Shabbat dinner on a Friday night, the limo taxi turned the wrong way for Jerusalem and our several destinations. The driver was going too fast for the winding roads above the city. He didn't intend to slow down. But he did stop three times and ordered two passengers out of the limo by waving what looked like a scimitar at them. Finally, only Mussaphir and I were left, leaving Jerusalem, the kibbutz and other "Fulbrighters" far behind. There are few roads in Israel and all of them are patrolled, but we didn't see any troops on Shabbat. The young Jordanian driver stopped once for gas and warned me not to leave the limo. By this time it was dark; there were no lights except for those in the gas station which obviously doubled as a "hash house." The smell wafted out across the night as about twenty men sat smoking and looking at the car. There was no place to run and hide. As we left the station, it seemed that we were on the way to Bethlehem and the Allenby Bridge, guarded on one side by Israelis and on the other side by Jordanians with machine guns.

Before we reached Bethlehem, I heard the sirens and knew the police or the Mossad was coming. This was just before I gathered my shawl around me, preparing to jump from the car. Three jeep-like vehicles loaded with Israelis in uniforms pulled the limo to the side of the road. When they took the driver from the car, I was amazed to see how small and young he was, but that was one big knife he carried.

He disappeared with the troops, and Mussaphir and I were never called to testify as to our "kidnapping." The incident never made the papers and we did not discuss it again.

While visiting the Bedouin in the desert, Mussaphir tried to sell me to a little man in a blue robe for 300 camels. The Bedouin was serious; I was not. Arie Shoval, our mentor, saved me from an unknown fate. I tried to avoid Mussaphir the remainder of our time in Israel.

For several years, he would send me a Christmas card, reminding me of how he had "saved" my life one Friday night.

* * *

From the time I learned to read, at about the age of three, my lifelong obsession has been King Arthur, Queen Guinevere and the Knights of the Round Table. Of course, Arthur was born in the fifth century in Britain of a Roman father and a British mother. Arturus, the bear (token of the Shawnee) united Britain and kept the peace for forty years, holding back waves of Irish, Danes and Norsemen. I had to find him. He was their symbol of defiance in face of the inevitable. I went to Scotland, toured Dumbarton, and hiked the Antonine wall and read the excavation reports on Camlon. Then, I went over to Gigha, off the Mull of Kentyre, island of my grandfather. There my ancestors fought "the giants" in ancient times. I found the tombstones of the sailors and teachers who left Gigha's treacherous waters to see what was across the ocean. I was the first Gilbreath to set foot on Gigha after Sara Gilbreath died in 1920. I was treated royally. Great Grandfather Hiram came to the United States to fight for the Union, and in the Civil War he received two medals for "exceptional bravery" presented by Abraham Lincoln on the field of Gettysburg.

But I did not find King Arthur. Instead I found his queen, Guinevere. In the small village of Meigle, Scotland, in an old stone structure that had been a former church and school, is the Meigle Stone. Legend has it that it covered the grave of Queen Guinevere, and that it was brought to Meigle from Strathclyde centuries ago. The heart of ancient Pictdom was Strathclyde and if Guinevere was buried there, she must have been a Pict. The women of Meigle believed this to be true and revered the stone. They see Guinevere as a powerful, ancient warrior queen, not "the wicked woman" of the French chansons.

So I wrote about Guinevere, but continued my search for King Arthur who married Guinevere, not for love, but for land and power.

When I returned to London, on a whim, I bought the last ticket on a plane to the Isle of Mann. No one except J. W. and Beverly would believe what happened to me there, but that did not alter the events as they unfolded.

It was raining and cold when I left London in August, so I wore a heavy jacket, shirt, sweater, jeans, hiking boots with wool socks and a shawl over all to keep warm. The trip by air was short, about 45 minutes, but oh, the changes in less than an hour away from London. Looking down as we landed in Wellington, I could see children playing in the ocean, blossoming plum trees, and people strolling along the strand. Perhaps I was overdressed.

I knew no one on the island and hoped that Travelers Aid could find me a bed and breakfast on the Strand. When I exited the back of the plane, I could see the desk at the end of the airport where Travelers Aid was manned by one person while another leaned on the counter.

As I approached, the one behind the desk asked the other, "Is she the one?"

I looked around the small airport and could see that I was the only one. Maybe I should quickly get back on the plane that was taxiing away for service.

"You're Barbara, aren't you?"

Oh, Lordy, what was this?

"Look out there, I've held the bus for fifteen minutes waiting for you."

There at the curb was a small jitney filled with laughing people waving for me to come and get on board. It was all open – no windows or doors to block my flight. Why not? If it was a conspiracy, what did it all mean?

David Knight picked up my little black carry-all, introducing himself and informing me that his wife's name was Barbara; she had tea waiting and had been expecting me for several days. She had been saving petrol stamps so we could look for King Arthur and had even alerted a stand-in cook to prepare breakfast and lunch for their six foster children while we went adventuring.

Honest!

The jitney drove into town to the train station on the Strand and excited tourists got off to take the small train to the 12th century castle on the other side of the island.

I could still jump off the bus and run.

Just then David said,

"Look down the street. There's Barbara with the kids. They want to meet you before they go back to school."

We drove down the block, I met the kids. Barbara and I had tea in the basement kitchen and planned to go adventuring. David had to work extra because he was a bus driver for the tourists.

A young boy had carried my bag to the turret room that Barbara had reserved for me. I could look out and see the whole east coast of Mann. Was this the island of the three queens? Was this where King Arthur's funeral boat came to rest? Had the queens cared for him when he was endangered or wounded? On a clear day, could I see the three ancient kingdoms of Britain as described in the Welsh annals.

To this day, I believe!

For three incredible days I was one of the queens of the island kingdom. The Knight family took me to a medieval festival that evening. Several years before I had competed in archery at an all-Indian pow-wow and had won an Oswego wampum necklace that I treasure.

Barbara urged me on to the archery contest saying, "We can use the big basket of food when you place second. The kids will cheer you on." They did; I won to great acclaim and we received a big basket of food.

I asked to see a Manx cat with no tail. One appeared suddenly. Where were the sheep with double horns? Here came a flock of them down the hill. Of course, Barbara was a Druid priestess. I believed.

The next day, we filled the car with petrol and took off for the western side of Mann. At the petrol station, the attendant commented to Barbara, "She came." And I nodded, "Yes, I came."

In less than an hour, we could see the ruins of the medieval castle, but that was not our destination. A small peninsula called the Calf of Mann was where archaeological excavations had been on going. There was St. Patrick's first church. The islanders claimed that the graves of Joseph of Arimathaea and his wife were just offshore. A single archaeologist was writing up his field report and unlocked the gate so we could explore the area.

"Just in time; I was leaving in an hour."

"I know," said Barbara and I believed.

She wouldn't go with me when I wanted to see the cave under St. Patrick's Church. She said that Guinevere was thrown into the snake pit there. The archaeologist said to take his flash light and be prepared to run from the ghost.

Into the cave and the utter darkness, I went, hoping St. Patrick had driven all the snakes from Mann as well as from Ireland. After 200 feet into the cave, it was cold, cold, cold. I could feel the sounds of the sea through my feet. I went further underground. I couldn't see the cave entrance. The rocks closed in. I panicked and ran out of there as fast as I could, stumbling and praying to St. Patrick and Guinevere, "Get me out of here."

The archaeologist took Barbara and me to his office and gave me a cup of coffee—I was shaking. Then, he let me read the excavation reports on the grave of a fifth century knight that had been recovered, complete with a five-foot sword that had been broken in two places.

That night in the turret room, I dreamed of King Arthur, snakes, Guinevere and black cats with no tails, but I felt refreshed in the morning. For breakfast, Barbara had made special biscuits with plums. When I left the island for London, the whole family came to the airport in the jitney to see me off. I couldn't wait to tell everyone about my quest to Mann.

When I finally returned to the United States after hiking Ireland, I wanted to send the Knight family something special. I ordered three large *Yahoo Cakes* in the shape of Texas and mailed them to Mann.

Weeks and months passed. I hoped they had eaten every bite and enjoyed.

Then, I received a very official looking letter from customs on the Isle of Mann. I was informed that no family by the name of Knight lived at that address on the island or anywhere on Mann. However, the cakes looked so good that the officials ate them at tea-time rather than return them to the United States in moldy condition.

***

The only place in all my travels that I would never hope to see again was South Korea. For three months, I listened to Korean scholars tell me how much they hated the United States and how we were personally responsible for the Korean conflict. Harry Truman had divided the Korean people at the 38th parallel and that had caused their major problem with North Korea.

I watched as women with no names were beasts of burden, pulling heavy carts through the crowded streets of Itewan. One woman had her legs switched, like she was a donkey, as she tried to maneuver a wagon the size of a small car along a sidewalk. The

Fulbrights were cheated, lied to, cursed, put up in burned-out hotels, in roach-filled rooms and led around to every Buddhist temple in the country. Getting off the plane, I was struck by a terrible stench of the country; likewise, the food which was usually fermented. During the meals, while others were eating, I would steal the dessert of watermelon. I survived Korea by eating stolen watermelon. I had watched them make kimchi on the sidewalk and wondered how anyone could eat it without being sick. A U.S. army general explained that in the Korean conflict, when taking a village, his troops would wear gas masks until it was determined that the smell they experienced was kimchi in old pots exploded by mortar fire and not poison gas.

On the plane coming home, with double pneumonia, I spoke with businessmen who also had a problem communicating with their Korean counterparts. Bids changed overnight, contracts were rewritten frequently, specifications revised until the original plans were unrecognizable. Then, everything was suddenly withdrawn and there was no deal at all. Teachers of English had their pay cut drastically without explanation. Yet they couldn't leave until they had fulfilled the time on their contracts.

J. W. and Me: The Small Town Texas Experience

The phones at the U.S. Embassy in Seoul were answered by Koreans who pretended not to understand English. Unlike the my time on the Fulbright to Israel, there would be no Fourth of July party. Instead, I hiked in the rain to the army compound to hear the *1812 Overture* and *God Bless America*. Back in Texas, I wrote the State Department about their representatives and the treatment of visitors. Of course, I received no answer from them. However, a year later I had the opportunity to voice my disdain and despair over the Korean experience when the two ambassadors met in Dallas—the Korean Ambassador to the United States and the returning U.S. Ambassador. In the open forum after their "diplomatic" speeches, I asked each if a requirement for their jobs was a course in how to be rude and arrogant to visiting scholars or was it merely a necessity for the job.

When they looked at me in shock, I left the room.

Oh, well I had been a goodwill ambassador to Mexico and I did get nominated to be the ambassador to Mexico. Obviously, I was not born to be a diplomat.

* * *

The Chinese government was interested in scholars from the United States to study their educational system. From Korea we went to China and a more cordial reception. The food, for one thing, was good and plentiful. I discovered that duck could be prepared in 100 different dishes, and I tried all of them, recovering the twenty-five pounds I had lost in Korea.

The "cultural revolution" was but a memory as we were shown the beauties of the forbidden city and Chinese gardens.

Returning to the hotel room after a visit to the countryside, our two young hosts were carefully reading letters sent to me while I was in Korea. They even checked out the books at the bottom of my suitcase and were returning everything to its place in the suitcase. Not in the least embarrassed at getting caught carefully snooping, they smiled and said in perfect English,

"We have brought you hot tea with two sugars, just the way you like it." They were extremely polite.

I smiled in return and graciously thanked them for their thoughtfulness.

They even provided for a massage and three therapists who eased my aching bones. The young man, held up by the two women, walked down my spine. It was wonderful.

On a visit to the university in Bejing we were not

permitted to speak to students or their professors. However, I was taken to several elementary schools where English is taught from Kindergarten through the fifth grade. At that time, students have the option to continue in English or take a third language for another three years. They study geography. And they have recess, too. I saw no fat Chinese. The school day in most countries begins at eight a.m. and ends at four or five p.m. Small wonder that our students, on a worldwide scale, are surpassed in science, math and reading comprehension, and some of them can't find Texas on a U.S. map.

* * *

Returning to Texas I researched the family tree to discover why I was in foster care for five or six years, I found part of my heritage with my Grandfather Crawford, a Native American. He loved horses and turquoise. Not only did I go to reservations as a kind of pilgrimage, but went to the All Nations Pow-Wow in Albuquerque. It was the experience of a lifetime. All tribes, including the Maoris and Mayans were represented: dancers, singers, drummers, all in costume, were performing. I could finally embrace all of my inheritance, Native American, Jewish, Scottish and Irish.

* * *

Many years ago, I taught a university course in the history of law. This is probably why my name was suggested for municipal judge. I have studied law codes from ancient to modern times. My doctoral dissertation was about an extra-legal institution in Mexico called the Acordada. It was similar in organization to the Texas Rangers. The Spanish crown had ordered the organization of the Santa Hermandad to bring order in the countryside of Castile. Then it had been carried to the New World to control the rural areas of Cuba before its transportation to Mexico. In the archives of Cuba, there must be a record of this transmission of the Santa Hermandad, which became the Acordada in the New World.

I needed to research this transmission in the Cuban Archives. The problem was getting to Cuba. Since the blockade and boycott, special permission for a license could be granted for musicians and sometimes for research. I applied to the U.S. government for a license. Four months later I received notification that the application was rejected. I called Washington three times and on the fourth call, I heard a sympathetic voice. I finally received permission for a week in Cuba to do research. Getting there was another problem. From Florida I flew to Cancun where the Cuban airline turned down everyone with a passport, except me. I had a license, but no one ever looked at it.

When I arrived in Cuba, I was the only person in a huge airport with lots of empty chairs and no taxis. The Japanese had arrived before me. It was absolutely black outside the terminal where two hours later, a poor, old 1956 Chevy picked me up.

I had a reservation at the only hotel with a swimming pool—water is a scarce commodity in Cuba; so it is necessary when making a reservation, to be sure that the hotel pool has water in it. Food is a scarce commodity. Medicine is a scarce commodity. Cuba manufactures medicine, but it is shipped to Latin America. Paper is scarce, gas is scarce. My French fries were rationed—exactly five to a hamburger.

But there was a swimming pool at the hotel where prostitution was a flourishing business. It was the pickup point for German, Japanese and Italian businessmen. And the women were gorgeous. There, I spoke with the local doctor who made more money (especially U.S. dollars) in the oldest profession, than she made doctoring. She assured me she was a very good doctor. Many women, heads of families, declared they were free of husbands who, thankfully, had left Cuba for Miami. This was a surprise. Many women support the Castros in spite of shortages.

The beaches were breathtaking – clean, blue and mostly empty. Cubans are not allowed at Veradero, the most beautiful beach in the world. A former economics professor served me lunch, on the veranda with an ocean view. He told me where I might find information on the Acordada, but the university was closed for the summer.

At the national library the roof leaked and I used my umbrella in the admissions area to keep dry. Worms nibbled at ancient documents for which I paid $25 to see each *legago* (bundle of documents). When I ran out of money, I couldn't see any more documents. I couldn't find enough material in the archives to expand a book on the Acordada.

Ancient cars don't go to the junk yard, they go to Cuba where cars and bicycles are tied together creatively with wire and twine.

There is no money to repair the 17th and 18th century churches nor the ancient Spanish structures along the harbor. When Pope John Paul II came, the fronts of the buildings were painted, but the sides and back were collapsing.

Two maids cleaned my room. They left me candy and begged me to take them to the United States.

Cuban cigars were expensive, but students from Harvard stuffed the pockets of their jackets with them and sailed through customs.

No one ever looked at my license in Cuba or upon reentering the United States.

* * *

I liked Peru so much that I did a film for cable that I called *Paths of Peru, a Short History*. Others have described Machu Pichu, but when I saw the Condor flying above the hitching post of the sun, I had to see it recorded. A young photographer took the best pictures of the site I've ever seen. Luis Martín narrated my description of the countryside. The former president of Peru, Belunde-Terry, assisted me in Lima, so I sent him a finished copy of the film.

In between trips, I also wrote *The American Story*, thirty one half-hour programs in a history series for educational purposes for the Dallas County Community College District. Friends of my mother would call me from Chicago to tell me about their kids learning history on Saturday morning by watching the series on

PBS.

My mother was my copyreader. She took care of the dogs when I went filming around the country, but as a former English teacher, she enjoyed correcting my scripts and advising me on grammar. She died one week before the first program aired on PBS. The Texas State House and Senate gave me a Texas flag and a nice citation, but I wish my mother could have seen the series she helped create.

Part V
Afterward

J. W. and Me: The Small Town Texas Experience

In nine years, the city of Heath had grown. J. W. still wanted to retire. I didn't realize until later that his eyes were failing. Then his wife became ill.

J. W. located a nice young man to be his assistant and get to know the town. He was involved in the church and was an "upstanding citizen." I loaned him a copy of a book by my favorite archaeologist. I had met Vendyl Jones in Israel on my first Fulbright, and we had walked most of Israel together. From being a Baptist preacher he had become a Jewish convert to Noah's principles.

Vendyl often spoke in my honor's class, *The Bible as History*. I invited Billy, our new sheriff, to hear this "pied piper" of American Archeology. I called Vendyl a "pied piper" because every time he spoke to my class, one or two students would follow him from the classroom and disappear to Israel and Vendyl's excavation. He had already discovered a vial of oil which had anointed the kings of Israel, and the incense in the cave of the column, which rabbis in Israel collected from him.

Billie came to hear Vendyl. He left the classroom, borrowed some money, resigned as police chief, said goodbye to his wife and left for Israel with Vendyl to seek the ashes of the red heifer.

J. W. and Me: The Small Town Texas Experience

On my third trip to Israel, I looked for Billie, but I never saw him again. Perhaps he is still in Israel.

We had a difficult time finding a replacement.

For nine years, Aileen, J. W. and I represented justice in Heath, and court had received commendations from Austin for the job we had done. J. W., as the first Chief of Police, should have received a medal. Instead, his son and I had to claim his picture from City Hall before it was discarded by a new "progressive" administration.

* * *

LizzyBeth. *Courtesy of Mary Ann Asberry.*

As I sit here writing, J. W.'s dog is sitting on my feet to make sure that I don't go anywhere without her. He called her Scotty, but that is no name for a funny, loving mutt with hair in her eyes, so I have called her LizzyBeth because she looks like a Lizzy. The Beth is to give her a little class. Lizzy was bequeathed to me when J. W. went into the nursing home.

The first week he signed himself into the home, I went to see him.

"Miss Barbara, could you go to my house and see to the little dog I just adopted? She's out there somewhere and runs from everyone." His son Johnny said "she was mistreated and won't come to just anyone."

How could I say no to J. W. ?

An hour later when I went to the bank, there was Johnny again.

"I'm going to close up Daddy's house. Why don't you come with me? He has a little dog there that needs a home."

If I hadn't just lost my dog Willie-Willie, and if my other dog, Alice the Woogie, hadn't needed a companion, and if I hadn't been driving the Woogie around with me wherever I went, and if Woogie and I had not already been to the doggie shelter where she hated every dog that she saw . . .

She growled at several of them. She ran and hid behind the car wheels when she looked at others brought outside for her inspection. We finally left the shelter after an afternoon of dog hunting and she went to sleep in the front seat of the car.

So we went with Johnny, and the Woogie ran free

in the fields enjoying the sunshine. We didn't see another dog. When it was time to go, I whistled for her. She came around the corner of J. W.'s house followed by a funny looking puppy...part golden retriever, part terrier, part cocker spaniel, built low to the ground on little legs with big paws and a lost look. Neither dog looked at me, but when I opened the car door, both dogs got in and curled up in the back seat.

Johnny, with a knowing look, said, "I think you just got a new dog."

When we got home, Alice the Woogie pushed the puppy into the swimming pool to baptize her and clean her up.

On that last cold day in March, I took off my shoes and went in the frigid water to retrieve our Lizzie. I couldn't stick her in the dryer, so I got a big towel and rubbed her dry while the Woogie sat in front of us wagging her tail. I did not know that Alice the Woogie had cancer. But she knew and made sure that I had a new protector when she went away.

Sometimes, I visit the nursing home with Lizzie and read pages of the book to J. W. for his approval. We laugh about the "old times" when he was the Chief of Police and I was the Judge of the Municipal Court in Heath, Texas.

Barbara V. Montgomery
Rockwall, Texas 2007

Galahad

Weary with years,
Faces of loved ones dimly remembered,
Only the vision remains.

Dead the gallant mount,
Dead the grey war dog,
So faithful and so fierce.

Night without stars,
Path without end,
Alone, with the bright challenge.

No more time,
To regret, to turn back,
Or even try again.

Sit quietly,
Death is near,
The question asked and answered.

Wonderer, seeker,
Did you not know?
It was the search itself?

B.V.M

J. W. and Me: The Small Town Texas Experience

Appendix I

The rebuilt Cedar Grove Christian Church, first established in 1875. The original building was also used as a school. *Courtesy of Mary Hanrahan.*

Cedar Grove Christian Church History

Cedar Grove Christian church was organized in 1875. It was a small frame building, 12x12, located on Old Glen Road near the Trinity River "bottom." It served the Glen Hill settlement, now under the water of Lake Ray Hubbard.

In 1882, the Rockwall School District furnished material for a one-room school on land donated by Glen Clark for as long as the school was in operation. This was the first black school in Rockwall County.

When the building was destroyed by fire in the summer of 1928, the church and school met under the cedar trees. Then Martha Roberts rented the church and school a house near the Glen Hill settlement. In

1930, Jody Chisolm offered land for a new church and in 1940 a new school building was constructed on land near the church given by John Martin.

Classes and worship were joined when the congregation moved into the new school house.

The congregation grew and a new sanctuary was completed in 1952. This church is on the hill overlooking I-30 and Horizon Road.

J. W. and Me: The Small Town Texas Experience

Appendix II

History of Glen Hill Chisolm Family Cemetery

Road marker for the historic Glen Hill Cemetery. *Courtesy of Mary Hanrahan.*

The Chisolms originated in the state of Georgia, deep in the heart of the south.

Twelve years before the slaves were freed, Mary Ann and Elizabeth, twin girls, were born to Violet Gardner Chisolm and Barney Chisolm.

Barney, being a slave, was sold away from his wife, Violet, and the twin girls. Barney was brought to this area by his new owners. Later, he received a message that his wife and twin girls were in or around the Henderson, Texas area. He prepared to go in search of his loved-ones.

Barney Chisolm found and retrieved his family, bringing them back to live in what is now Rockwall County, then Kaufman County. He purchased 87 ½ acres south of the city of Rockwall, then considered backwoods, and the bottom, meaning the East Fork of the Trinity River bottom, presently known as Lake Shore Property; Lake Ray Hubbard. The Glen Hill Chisolm Family Cemetery is located in the center of this vast acreage, now divided by Farm Road 740.

This backwoods settlement of ex-slaves served as home for several of Barney's grandchildren, great-grandchildren and great, great-grandchildren as late as 1993. There is one grandchild surviving, Maude Martin Terrell of Los Angeles. Two acres still remain from the estate. The two acres serve as the Chisolm Family Cemetery (Glen Hill).

The family is trying to make the Chisolm Family Cemetery a Historic Landmark. It is only proper that we restore and landmark the cemetery out of love and respect to the generations that have gone on before us. From them we have inherited much, and because of them our lives have been fruitful.

Carol Moton Hawkins

The journey of a thousand miles begins with one step.

The Glen Hill Cemetery. The oldest known person's grave is of a slave born in 1818. *Courtesy of Mary Hanrahan.*

www.ingramcontent.com/pod-product-compliance
Lightning Source LLC
Chambersburg PA
CBHW050654160426
43194CB00010B/1933